ADOBE ILLUSTRATOR

FOR BEGINNERS 2023

CREATE STUNNING DESIGNS EFFORTLESSLY

by

MARY LAMBERTH

COPYRIGHT

Printed in the United States of America

© 2023 by Mary Lamberth

New Age Publishing

USA | UK | CANADA

TABLE OF CONTENTS

INTRODUCTION

Adobe Illustrator is an essential tool for anyone working in graphic design or digital illustration. It is a user-friendly application that provides powerful tools to help you create stunning designs. With Adobe Illustrator, you can create intricate illustrations and graphics with ease.

The software's interface is intuitive, making it easy for beginners to start. It provides a range of templates and tutorials that can help you create professional designs even with little experience.

One of the critical benefits of Adobe Illustrator is its ability to create vector graphics. Vector graphics are made up of shapes and lines, and unlike raster images, they can be scaled up or down without losing quality. This makes them perfect for creating logos, icons, and other designs that need to be resized.

In addition to vector graphics, Adobe Illustrator offers a range of other features. You can add text to your designs, use gradients and patterns, and work with different color palettes. You can also use the software to create print-ready designs and export your work in various file formats.

Overall, Adobe Illustrator is a powerful and versatile tool for anyone working in graphic design or digital illustration. It's an essential part of any designer's toolkit and can help you create professional-looking designs quickly and easily.

PART 1 → HOW TO START USING ADOBE ILLUSTRATOR

To start using Adobe Illustrator is easier than it seems.

Firstly, you need to get Adobe Illustrator by purchasing a subscription from Adobe's website or downloading a free trial version of the software to test it out.

Once you have purchased or downloaded the software, follow the installation instructions to install Adobe Illustrator on your computer. Open the software and proceed to explore the interface.

STARTING A NEW DOCUMENT

First, you should see a window asking you to create a new document or open an existing one.

There are different custom sizes of documents you can easily click to start a new document. Also, you can easily access recent documents at the bottom of this window.

Now, click "Create New" to create a new document. A new window opens for you to set how you want your document to be.

In the New Document dialog box that appears, you can choose the settings for your new document. You can give your document a name and select the document's size, orientation, units, and color mode. You can also choose a preset size, such as A4 or Letter.

As a beginner, give your document a name. Change the measurement to inches and set the width to 12 and height to 9. Ensure the orientation is a landscape, and the color mode is RGB. Click "Create" after choosing your settings.

You are then presented with the Adobe Illustrator interface, where you can work and bring your imagination into reality.

FAMILIARIZING YOURSELF WITH THE INTERFACE

The interface of Adobe Illustrator is designed to provide a user-friendly and intuitive experience, with various tools and features that make it easier to create vector graphics.

The Adobe Illustrator interface is divided into several key areas:

1. Menu Bar: The Menu Bar is at the top of the screen and contains various menus such as File, Edit, Object, Type, View, Window, and Help. These menus provide access to various functions, features, and options within Illustrator. For example, the File menu allows you to create, open, and save documents, while the Object menu enables you to modify, group, and align objects.

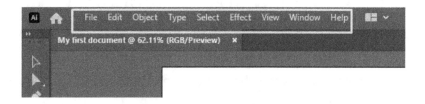

2. Tool Panel: The Tool Panel is located on the left side of the workspace and contains various tools for

creating, editing, and manipulating vector objects. These tools include the Selection, Pen, Type, and Shape tools. Each tool has its own set of options and settings, which can be accessed through the Control Panel.

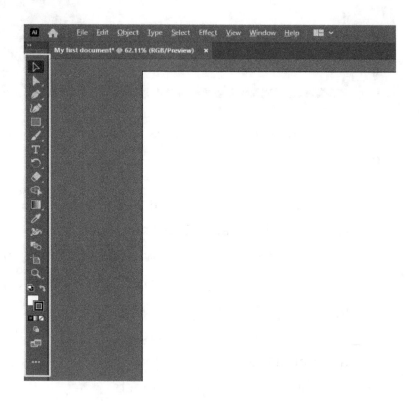

3. Document Window: The Document Window is the main area where you create and edit your vector artwork. The Document Window displays the canvas or artboard where you can create and arrange your objects. You can create multiple artboards within a single document, which can help create multiple versions of your design.

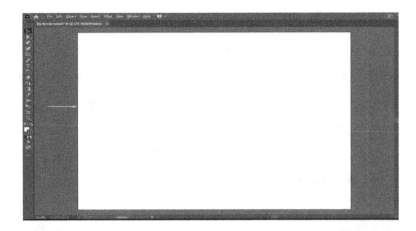

4. Panels: Panels are located on the right side of the workspace and provide access to additional tools, functions, and options. Panels can be used to adjust colors, create gradients, manage layers, and more. Some of the most commonly used panels include the Layers panel, the Color panel, and the Gradient panel.

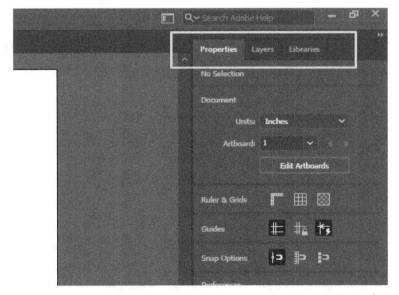

In addition to these critical areas, Adobe Illustrator provides various keyboard shortcuts, contextual menus, and customization options to make your workflow more efficient and productive. For example, you can customize the Tool Panel to show only the tools you use most frequently or create custom keyboard shortcuts for often-used functions.

Overall, the Adobe Illustrator interface is designed to provide a robust and intuitive environment for creating stunning vector graphics, illustrations, and typography. With its wide range of tools and features, Illustrator is a versatile and essential tool for any designer or artist.

SAVING A DOCUMENT

It is recommended to save your Illustrator documents frequently as you work on them to avoid losing your progress in case of any unexpected errors or crashes.

To save a document in Adobe Illustrator, you can follow these steps:

1. Click on the "File" menu in the top left corner of the screen.

2. Select "Save" or "Save As" from the drop-down menu.
3. If you are saving the document for the first time, select "Save As" and choose the location where you want to save the file.
4. Give your file a name and select the format you want to save it in. Illustrator files have the extension ".ai".

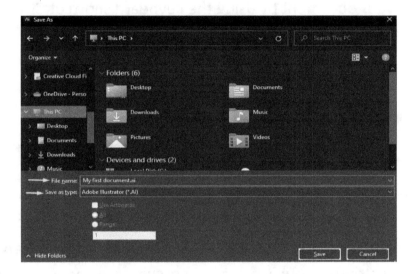

5. If you want to save a copy of the file in a different format, such as a JPEG or PDF, you can select the format from the "Save as type" drop-down menu.

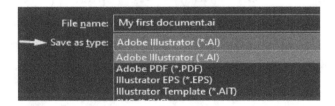

6. Click "Save" to save the file.

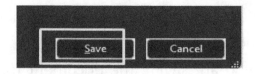

7. A dialogue box may pop up; click "Ok".

To ensure your document is regularly saved, click on "File" and select "Save" at regular intervals. Alternatively, save your document by using the keyboard shortcut Ctrl + S.

SETTING UP A WORKSPACE

In Adobe Illustrator, a workspace is a specific arrangement of panels, menus, and tools organized to help you efficiently complete a particular task or workflow. Illustrator comes with various pre-made workspaces, such as Essentials, Typography, and Layout, but you can also customize your workspace to suit your individual needs and preferences.

To access the pre-made workspaces, go to the top menu bar and click on Window > Workspace. You can select the workspace that best fits your current task.

To customize your workspace

If you want to customize a workspace or create a new one, you can drag panels around, collapse or expand them, and even create custom toolbars by going to Window > Toolbars > New Toolbar.

Once you have your workspace set up, save it by going to Window > Workspace > New Workspace. Give the new workspace a name and click "OK". This allows you to easily switch between different workspaces depending on what you're working on.

BASIC TOOLS AND THEIR FUNCTIONS

Adobe Illustrator is a powerful vector-based design software with a wide range of tools and features to help you create and edit graphics, illustrations, logos, and more.

However, you can know the names of these tools by hovering your mouse over each tool, and then the name is displayed. To use any of these tools, click on it and apply the tool on the document window.

Also, be aware that some of these tools carry other tools in them. For instance, the Rectangle tool has the Ellipse Tool, Polygon Tool, Star Tool, and Line Segment tool in it, as shown below. To display other tools in a tool, click and hold the tool till other tools appear.

Here are some essential tools and their functions in Adobe Illustrator:

1. Selection Tool (V): This is the default tool in Illustrator and is used to select, move, and resize objects in your document.

2. Direct Selection Tool (A): This tool selects individual anchor points or paths of a selected object to make specific changes to the shape or path.

3. Pen Tool (P): This tool creates and edits anchor points and paths to create custom shapes, lines, and curves.

4. Type Tool (T): This tool adds and edits text in your document. You can choose from various text options, including font, size, style, and alignment.

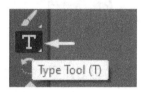

5. Shape Tools: Illustrator comes with a range of shape tools, including Rectangles, Rounded Rectangles, Ellipse, Polygon, and Star. These tools are used to create basic shapes that can be customized with colors, gradients, and strokes.

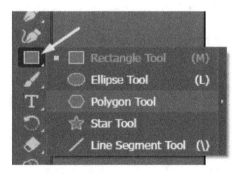

6. Paintbrush Tool (B): This tool creates freehand strokes with customizable brush sizes, shapes, and opacity.

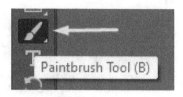

Paintbrush Tool (B)

7. Eraser Tool (Shift + E): This tool removes parts of a selected object or path.

Eraser Tool (Shift+E)

8. Eyedropper Tool (I): This tool is used to sample and select colors from an existing object or image in your document.

Eyedropper Tool (I)

9. Gradient Tool (G): This tool is used to create and apply gradients to selected objects, paths, or text.

Gradient Tool (G)

These are just some of the essential tools and their functions in Adobe Illustrator. You can create various designs and illustrations in Illustrator by mastering these tools. We will be using these tools as we learn to use Adobe Illustrator.

Changing the appearance of the toolbar

You can change the look of your toolbar from basic to advanced. When you switch to advanced, you are presented with more tools to work with in Adobe Illustrator.

To change from basic to advanced, Click the "Window" menu, click Toolbars, and choose "Advanced". You should then have a new look with more tools for your use.

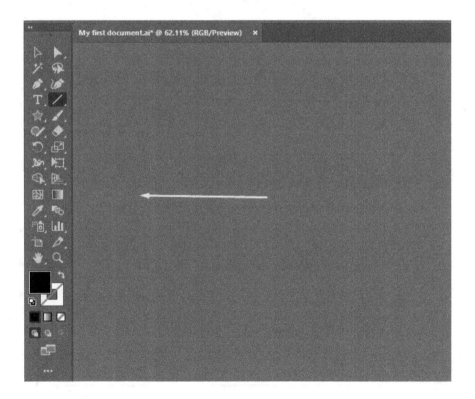

PART 2 → DRAWING AND EDITING OBJECTS IN ADOBE ILLUSTRATOR

Adobe Illustrator is a powerful vector-based design software that allows you to create and edit various objects, such as shapes, paths, and lines.

BASIC SHAPES AND LINES

Here are some basic shapes and lines you can create in Adobe Illustrator:

Shapes:

1. Rectangle Tool: Grab this tool as described earlier. Use this tool to draw a rectangular shape on the document window. Hold down the Shift key while dragging to draw a square. *Remember to click the* **Selection Tool** *after using any tool. The Selection Tool is the default tool in Adobe Illustrator.*

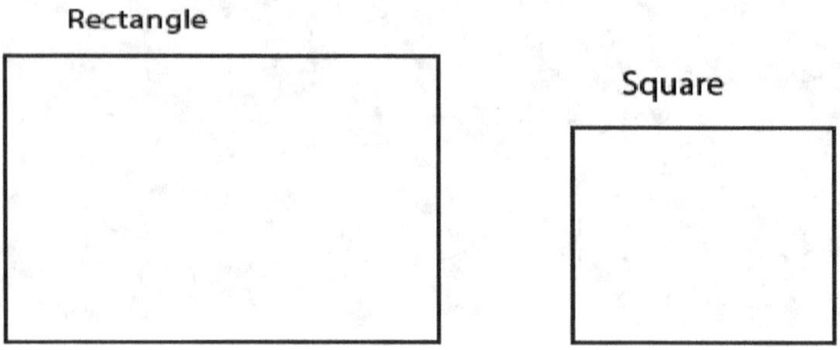

Rectangle

Square

2. Ellipse Tool: We use this tool to draw circular or elliptical shapes. Hold down the Shift key while dragging to draw a perfect circle.

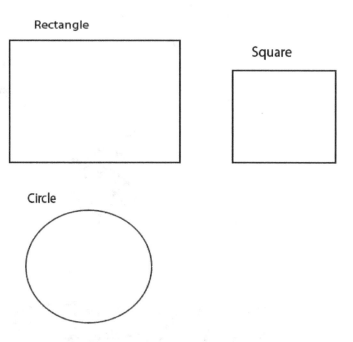

Rectangle

Square

Circle

3. Polygon Tool: We use this tool to draw shapes with multiple sides, such as triangles, pentagons, and hexagons.

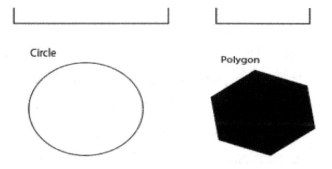

Circle

Polygon

4. Star Tool: We use this tool to draw stars with customizable numbers of points.

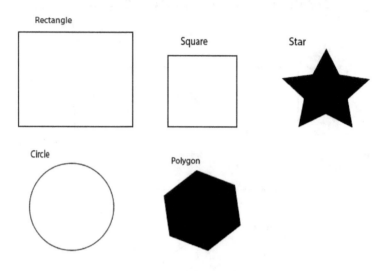

Lines:

1. Line Segment Tool: We use this tool to draw straight lines. Hold down the Shift key while dragging to draw a perfectly horizontal or vertical line.
2. Arc Tool: We use this tool to draw arcs and curves.
3. Spiral Tool: We use this tool to draw spirals with a customizable number of turns and spacing.

4. Rectangular Grid Tool: We use this tool to create grids with a customizable number of rows and columns.

MODIFYING SHAPES

Modifying shapes in Adobe Illustrator can be done in several ways depending on one's motive. Here are some of the most common methods:

Using the Selection Tool

The Selection Tool allows you to adjust the size, position, and rotation of your shapes.

Selecting objects: After drawing a shape, click the Selection Tool and click on the shape you wish to select. Once you click your shape with the Selection Tool, you should see a bounding box around the shape.

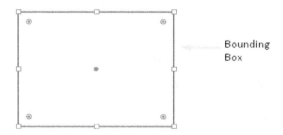

Bounding Box

To select multiple objects, click and drag a marquee around them. You can also hold down the Shift key while clicking to add objects to your selection.

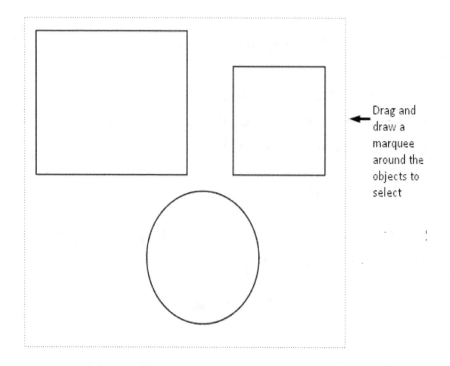

Drag and draw a marquee around the objects to select

Moving objects: Once an object or multiple objects are selected, you can move them by clicking and dragging with the Selection Tool.

Resizing objects: You can resize objects by clicking and dragging any of the bounding box handles that appear when an object is selected. Hold down the Shift key while dragging to constrain the object's proportions.

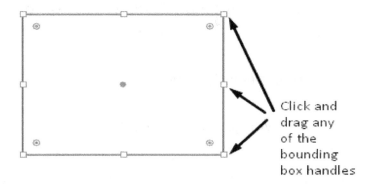

Click and drag any of the bounding box handles

Rotating objects: To rotate an object, hover your mouse over one of the corners of the bounding box until the rotation cursor appears, then click and drag to rotate. Hold down the Shift key to constrain the rotation angle.

Duplicating objects: You can duplicate an object by selecting it and then holding down the Alt key while dragging. This will create a copy of the object.

Grouping objects: You can group multiple objects by selecting them and then using the Group command when you click the Object menu or the keyboard shortcut Ctrl + G. This allows you to move and transform the objects as a single unit.

Locking objects: To prevent accidental movement or modification of an object, you can lock it by selecting it and then using the Lock command when you click the Object menu or the keyboard shortcut Ctrl + 2. You can unlock objects using the same commands.

By mastering the Selection Tool, you can work more efficiently and precisely in Illustrator.

Using the Direct Selection Tool

This tool allows you to select and modify individual anchor points and line segments in your shape. You can double-click and drag on an anchor point to move it or double-click and drag on a line segment to adjust its curvature.

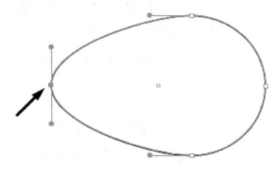

Adding color to a shape

You need to add color to make your shape look beautiful and appealing to the eye.

To add color to a shape, you can follow these steps:

1. Select the shape you want to color with the Selection Tool.
2. Open the Color panel by going to Window > Color or pressing the "F6" key on your keyboard.

3. Choose a color from the Color panel, or use the Eyedropper tool to sample a color from elsewhere in your document.

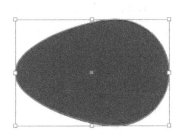 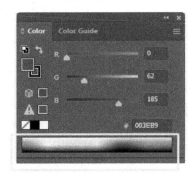

4. Close the Color panel by clicking on the "X" button at the top right corner of the panel.

Alternatively, you can use the following method to apply a gradient or pattern fill to a shape:

1. Select the shape you want to fill.
2. Open the Gradient panel by going to Window > Gradient or pressing the "Ctrl + F9" keys on your keyboard.
3. Choose a gradient type from the Gradient panel, or click on the Gradient swatch to create a new gradient.

4. Adjust the gradient stops and colors as desired.
5. To apply a pattern fill, open the Swatches panel by going to Window > Swatches or pressing the "F5" key on your keyboard.
6. Choose a pattern swatch from the Swatches panel, or click on the Swatches panel menu and select "Open Swatch Library" to browse more options.
7. Click on the Fill color swatch in the Color panel and select "Pattern" to apply the chosen pattern to the selected shape.

Using the Pathfinder Panel

This panel provides various tools for combining, dividing, and trimming shapes. You can use it to create complex shapes by combining simple ones.

Combine your shapes the way you want them to be.

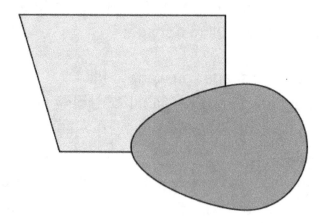

Select the shapes and go to Window > Pathfinder. Once the panel opens, choose from the various options how you want your new shape to be.

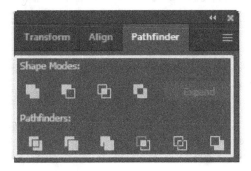

In the image below, the "Unite" shape mode was chosen.

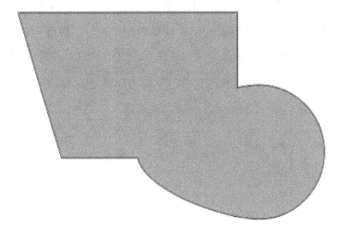

You can easily create more complex and detailed illustrations by mastering the different shape modification techniques in Illustrator. So, explore more by creating and manipulating different shapes you can think of.

DRAWING AND EDITING PATHS

We will use the Pen Tool to draw paths and the Direct Selection Tool to edit paths in Adobe Illustrator.

Here are the steps to draw and edit paths:

Drawing paths:

1. Select the Pen Tool from the toolbar.
2. Click once on the artboard to create the first anchor point of your path.
3. Move your mouse to a new location and click again to create a second anchor point. This will create a straight line segment between the two points.
4. Continue to add anchor points and click and drag to create curved segments as needed to complete your path.

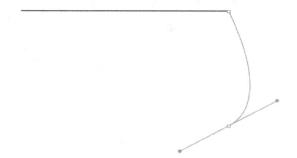

5. To close your path, move your mouse over the first anchor point until a small circle appears next to the Pen Tool icon, then click to close the path.

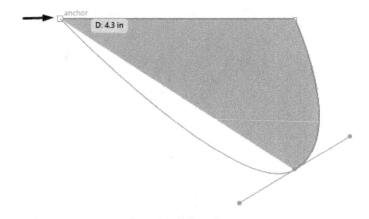

6. Below is the result of my drawing.

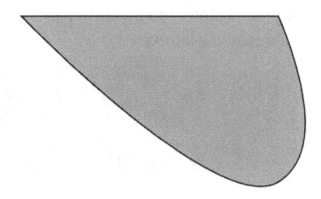

Editing paths:

1. Select the Direct Selection Tool from the toolbar.
2. Click on an anchor point to select it. Handles will appear on either side of the point.
3. Click and drag on a handle to adjust the curve of the path segment connected to the anchor point.

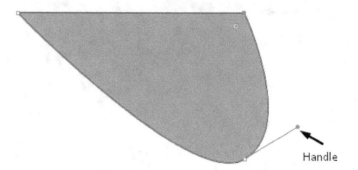

Handle

4. To convert a smooth anchor point to a corner point, select the anchor point with the Direct Selection Tool, then click the Convert Selected Anchor Points to Corner button in the Control panel at the right-hand side of the interface.

5. To convert a corner anchor point to a smooth point, select the anchor point with the Direct Selection Tool, then click the Convert Selected Anchor Points to Smooth button in the Control panel.

6. To add an anchor point to a path, select the Pen Tool and click on the path where you want to add the new point.
7. To delete an anchor point from a path, select the Direct Selection Tool and, click on the anchor point you want to delete, then press the Delete key.
8. To adjust the width of a path, select the Width Tool from the toolbar and click and drag on the path where you want to adjust the width.

These are the basic steps to draw and edit paths in Adobe Illustrator. With practice, you can master the Pen Tool and create complex shapes and designs.

ARRANGING OBJECTS

Arranging objects is a crucial part of creating a well-designed composition. It may be required of you to place an object on another. Here are some tips on how to arrange objects in Illustrator:

1. To bring an object to the front of the stack, select it and then go to Object > Arrange > Bring to Front or use the shortcut "Ctrl + Shift +]" (Windows) or "Command + Shift +]" (Mac). In the image below, the star is above the other shape.

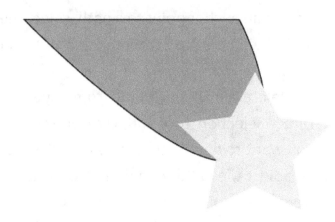

2. To send an object to the back of the stack, select it and then go to Object > Arrange > Send to Back or use the shortcut "Ctrl + Shift + [" (Windows) or "Command + Shift + [" (Mac).

3. To move an object up or down one layer in the stack, select it and then go to Object > Arrange > Bring Forward or Send Backward, respectively, or use the shortcuts "Ctrl +]" and "Ctrl + [" (Windows) or "Command +]" and "Command + [" (Mac).

4. To align multiple objects horizontally or vertically, select them and then use the Align panel (Window > Align) to choose the desired alignment option.

5. To group multiple objects together, select them and then go to Object > Group or use the shortcut "Ctrl + G" (Windows) or "Command + G" (Mac).

6. To ungroup a group of objects, select the group and then go to Object > Ungroup or use the shortcut

"Shift + Ctrl + G" (Windows) or "Shift + Command + G" (Mac).

7. To lock or unlock an object, select it and then go to Object > Lock or Object > Unlock or use the shortcuts "Ctrl + 2" and "Ctrl + Alt + 2" (Windows) or "Command + 2" and "Command + Option + 2" (Mac).

By mastering these techniques, you'll be able to create complex designs easily and precisely.

ARRANGING OBJECTS USING THE LAYERS PANEL

Working with layers in Adobe Photoshop allows you to organize, edit, and manipulate different parts of an image separately.

To rearrange your shapes, you can use the Layers panel, which can be accessed through Window > Layer if it is not already open.

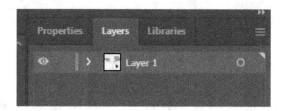

By default, all your objects will be on the same layer. To separate them, select one object/shape with the Selection

Tool and cut it using Ctrl or Command + X. Then, create a new layer by clicking the "New Layer" icon and paste the shape onto it using Ctrl or Command + V. You can then rename the layers if you wish.

Keep in mind that the arrangement of layers affects the order of shapes. To move a shape to the front, drag its layer up to the top. If two shapes are on top of each other, click and hold on their layers in the Layers panel and drag them to switch positions. This technique allows you to control the arrangement of your objects even if they are on the same layer.

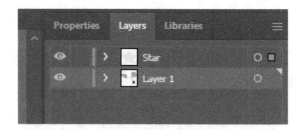

Here are some tips for working with layers:

1. Creating a new layer: To create a new layer, go to the Layers panel and click on the "Create New Layer" icon at the bottom of the panel. You can also use the shortcut key "Ctrl+L" (Windows) or "Cmd+L" (Mac).

2. Renaming layers: Double-click the layer name in the Layers panel to rename a layer and type in a new name.

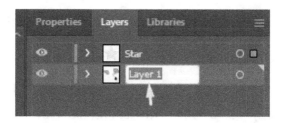

3. Reordering layers: To reorder layers, click and drag the layer to the desired position in the Layers panel.

4. Locking and hiding layers: You can lock or hide layers by clicking on the lock or eye icons next to the layer name in the Layers panel. This is useful for preventing accidental editing of specific elements or decluttering your workspace.

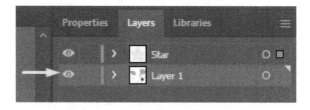

Overall, layers in Adobe Illustrator are a powerful tool for organizing and manipulating your artwork. Mastering these techniques allows you to create more efficient workflows and complex and dynamic designs.

NAVIGATING AND ZOOMING IN/OUT

As you work with various shapes and objects, you might need to move around or zoom in/out to make your work perfect.

Navigating and zooming in/out in Adobe Illustrator can be done using various methods. Here are some common ways to navigate and zoom in/out in Adobe Illustrator:

1. Hand Tool: To navigate around the artboard, select the Hand Tool (shortcut: H) and drag the artboard to move it in any direction.

2. Zoom Tool: To zoom in or out on the artboard, select the Zoom Tool (shortcut: Z) and click on the artboard to zoom in or Alt + click to zoom out.

3. Navigator Panel: The Navigator panel allows you to zoom in and out on the artboard and quickly navigate to different areas of the artboard. To open the Navigator panel, go to Window > Navigator or press Ctrl + Shift + F.

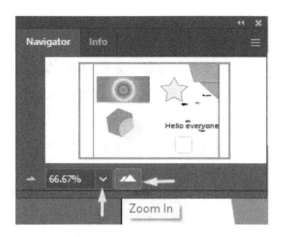

4. Zoom Slider: The Zoom slider is located at the bottom of the document window and allows you to zoom in and out by dragging the slider.

5. Keyboard Shortcuts: As mentioned earlier, you can also use keyboard shortcuts to zoom in and out of the artboard. To zoom in, press Ctrl + + (Windows) or Command + + (Mac). To zoom out, press Ctrl + - (Windows) or Command + - (Mac).

By using these different methods of navigating and zooming in/out, you can quickly and efficiently work on your design projects in Adobe Illustrator.

EXERCISE

This exercise is designed to help you practice drawing and editing objects in Adobe Illustrator. As you become more comfortable with these techniques, you can experiment with more complex designs and effects.

1. Create a new document: Open Adobe Illustrator and create a new document. Choose a size and orientation that suits your needs.
2. Draw a basic shape: Use the Shape Tool to draw a basic shape, such as a rectangle, circle, or triangle.
3. Add anchor points: Click on the shape with the Pen Tool to add anchor points. Use the Direct Selection Tool to move the anchor points and adjust the shape.
4. Draw a custom shape: Use the Pen Tool to draw a custom shape. Click and drag to create a line and then click and drag again to create a curve. Add anchor points and adjust the shape as needed.
5. Use the Pathfinder tool: Draw two shapes and overlap them. Select both shapes and click on the

Pathfinder Tool. Choose an option, such as Unite or Minus Front, to merge or subtract the shapes.

6. Use the Transform tool: Select a shape and click on the Transform Tool. Adjust the settings to scale, rotate, or skew the shape.

PART 3 → WORKING WITH TEXT IN ADOBE ILLUSTRATOR

Adobe Illustrator is a powerful tool for working with text, allowing you to create and manipulate text in various ways.

CREATING AND EDITING TEXT

To create text in Adobe Illustrator, follow these steps:

1. Select the Type tool: Click on the Type tool in the toolbar on the left side of the screen.

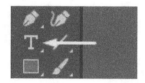

2. Click on the artboard: Click on the artboard where you want to add text.
3. Start typing: Begin typing the text you want to add.

Hello everyone!!!

4. Adjust font and size: Select your text with the Selection Tool. Click the Properties panel on the right-hand side of the interface or go to Window >

Properties. You can then use the panels under the Properties panel to manipulate your text. Use the Character panel to adjust the text's font, size, and other formatting options.

5. Add color to the text: Use the Appearance panel to change the color of the text.

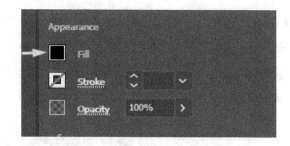

6. Align the text: Use the Paragraph and Align panels to align the text to the left, right, center, or justify it.

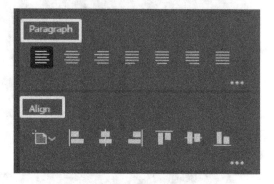

7. Adjust spacing: Use the Character panel to adjust the spacing between letters or words.

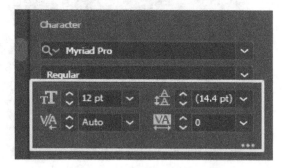

8. Move the text: Use the Selection tool to move the text to a different location on the artboard.

Hello everyone!!!

9. Save your work: Save your document to keep your changes.

Overall, creating and editing text in Adobe Illustrator is a straightforward process. Once you have added your text, you can adjust the formatting and placement to achieve the desired effect. Experiment with different fonts, sizes, and formatting options to create unique and eye-catching typography.

TEXT EFFECTS

Text effects help to enhance the appearance of your typography. You can have your texts in different shades and forms in Adobe Illustrator. Here are some widespread text effects you can use:

1. Drop shadow: A drop shadow adds depth to your text by creating a shadow behind the letters. To add a drop shadow, select your text and go to Effect > Stylize > Drop Shadow. A dialogue box is displayed, allowing you to adjust and choose a color for your style. Click "OK" when you are done.

2. Extrude and Bevel: A bevel and emboss effect adds a 3D look to your text by creating a raised, beveled edge. To add a bevel and emboss effect, select your text and go to Effect > 3D > Extrude and Bevel. A dialogue box is displayed, which will allow you to manipulate and choose a color for your style. Take your time to understand how to use this style. Click "OK" when you are done.

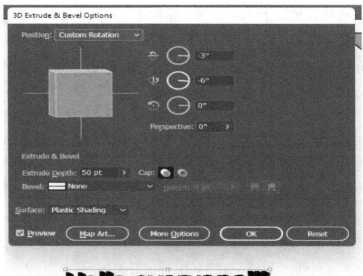

3. Warp: The Warp tool allows you to bend and distort your text in various ways, such as arching, bulging, or twisting. Select your text and go to Effect > Warp to use the Warp tool. A dialogue box is displayed, allowing you to adjust your style. Click "OK" when you are done.

4. Outline stroke: An outline stroke creates a border around your text, making it stand out from the background. Select your text to add an outline stroke, go to the Appearance panel, and then choose Stroke. Choose a color for the stroke and set a weight.

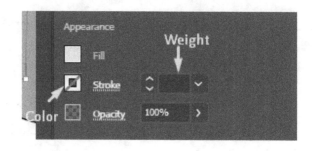

5. Distort and Transform: The Distort and Transform effects allow you to distort and transform your text in various ways, such as skewing, twisting, or scaling. To use these effects, select your text and go to Effect > Distort and Transform. Explore the different options under Distort and Transform.

Overall, using text effects in Adobe Illustrator can add a new level of depth and interest to your typography.

Experiment with different effects to create unique and eye-catching designs.

OTHER TYPOGRAPHY TOOLS

Typography tools help you create and manipulate text. Here are some of the key typography tools you can use in Illustrator:

1. Type tool: The Type Tool allows you to create and edit the text in your document, as discussed above.

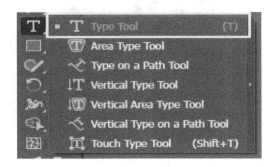

2. Character panel: The Character panel allows you to adjust the font, size, style, and other formatting options for your text.

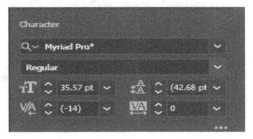

3. Paragraph panel: The Paragraph panel allows you to adjust the alignment, spacing, and other formatting options for paragraphs of text.

4. Area type Tool: The Area type Tool allows you to create a block of text within a defined shape. To access this tool, click and hold the Text tool.

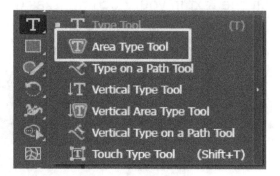

5. Type on a Path Tool: The Type on a Path Tool allows you to add text along a curved or straight path.

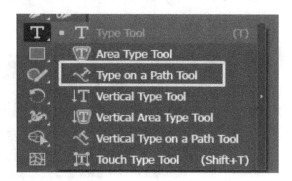

6. Touch Type Tool: The Touch Type Tool allows you to manipulate individual characters within a block of text, such as resizing or rotating them.

Overall, using typography tools in Adobe Illustrator can help you create professional-quality designs with visually appealing typography. Experiment with different tools and options to find the best combination for your design needs.

EXERCISE

This exercise is designed to help you practice working with text in Adobe Illustrator. As you become more comfortable with these techniques, you can experiment with more complex designs and effects.

1. Create a new document: Open Adobe Illustrator and create a new document. Choose a size and orientation that suits your needs.

2. Add text: Use the Type Tool to add a text box to the document and type in a simple phrase or sentence.
3. Choose a font: Click on the text box and choose a font from the Font menu. Experiment with different fonts until you find one that suits your design.
4. Adjust font size and color: Use the Character panel to adjust the font size and color. You can also adjust the letter spacing and line spacing to create a more visually pleasing design.
5. Add a stroke and fill: Click on the text box, go to Object > Expand, and then Object > Ungroup. Click on the text again and choose Object > Path > Outline Stroke. This will convert the text to a vector shape that you can modify. Use the Fill and Stroke tools to add color and strokes to the text.
6. Apply a text effect: Choose Effect, Distort & Transform, then choose a text effect such as Warp or Shear. Adjust the settings to create a unique text effect.

PART 4 → ADDING COLOR AND EFFECTS IN ADOBE ILLUSTRATOR

Color and effects are essential elements of graphic design, and they can be used to enhance the visual impact of your artwork.

FILLS AND STROKES

Fills and strokes are two important design elements in Adobe Illustrator that can be used to add color, shape, and definition to your artwork.

Fills:

- Fills refer to the color or pattern applied to the interior of a shape or object.

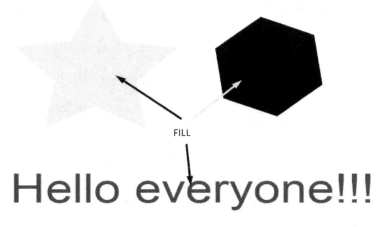

FILL

Hello everyone!!!

- To apply a fill, select the object or shape and choose a color or pattern from the Swatches panel or the Color panel. You can access the Swatches panel by going to Window > Swatches.

 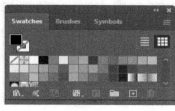

- You can also create a custom fill by going to Object > Pattern > Make.
- Fills can be adjusted in various ways, including changing the opacity, blending mode, and gradient direction.

Strokes:

- Strokes refer to the outline or border of a shape or object.

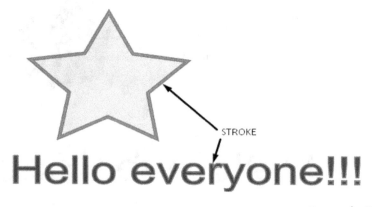

STROKE

Hello everyone!!!

- To apply a stroke, select the object or shape and choose a color by clicking the Stroke color button in the Appearance panel.

- You can increase the thickness of the stroke by inputting a value in the Stroke weight box.

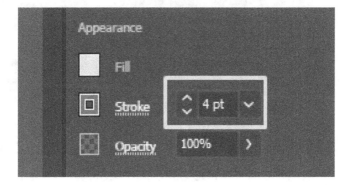

- You can also adjust the stroke properties, such as the cap style, corner style, and dash pattern, by clicking on Stroke in the Appearance panel. Click Dashed Line in the stroke properties to create a border or an outline.

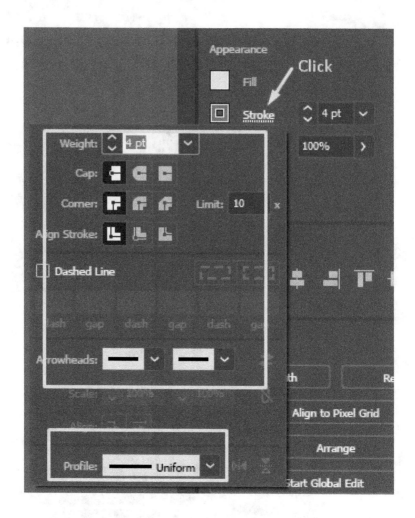

- Strokes can be applied to both closed and open paths and can be used to create various effects, such as outlines, frames, and borders.

When using fills and strokes in your designs, it's important to consider the overall look and feel you want to achieve. Experiment with different colors, patterns, and stroke styles to see what works best for your artwork. You can also use fills and strokes in combination with other design elements, such as gradients, textures, and effects, to create more complex and dynamic designs.

COLOR MODES

Color modes are important concepts in graphic design and digital art. Here's an overview of what they are and how they differ:

Color modes:

- Color modes refer to the different ways that color can be represented in digital images.
- The two most common color modes are RGB and CMYK.
- RGB (Red, Green, Blue) is used for digital images and is based on how light is projected from a screen. This mode is used for creating designs that will be viewed on a screen, such as websites, mobile apps, and social media.
- CMYK (Cyan, Magenta, Yellow, Black) is used for print images based on how ink is absorbed into the paper. This mode is used for creating designs that will be printed, such as business cards, brochures, and posters.

In Adobe Illustrator, you can select the color mode and model for your document by going to File > New and choosing the appropriate settings in the New Document dialog box.

To change the color mode and model for an existing document, go to File > Document Color Mode and select either RGB or CMYK.

GRADIENTS

Gradients are a powerful design tool that allows you to create smooth transitions between two or more colors.

Here's how you can create gradients in Illustrator:

1. Select the object you want to apply the gradient to. This can be a shape or a text object.

2. Open the Gradient panel by going to Window > Gradient.

3. Choose the type of gradient you want to use. There are several gradient types to choose from, including linear, radial, and freeform gradients.

4. Click Edit Gradient in the Gradient panel. Then, you should have a line you can manipulate on your shape.

5. Double-click the nodes on the line to change the color in your shape. You can choose colors from the Color panel that appears.

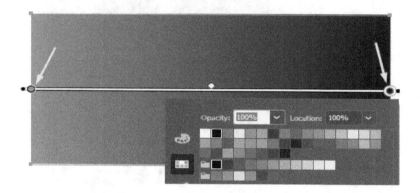

6. Adjust the gradient angle or position if necessary. For linear gradients, you can adjust the angle of the gradient using the Angle field in the Gradient panel. For radial gradients, you can adjust the position of the gradient by dragging the center point.

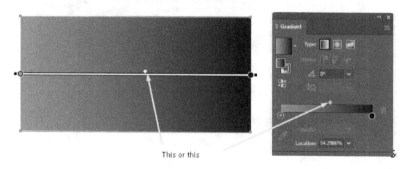

This or this

7. Fine-tune the gradient using the Gradient Tool. The Gradient Tool allows you to adjust the gradient by dragging the gradient slider, adjusting the midpoint, or adding color stops.

8. Save the gradient as a swatch if you want to reuse it later. To do this, select the object with the gradient, and drag it to the Swatches panel.

In addition to these basic steps, Illustrator also offers advanced gradient features, such as transparency and blending modes, that can be used to create complex and unique gradients.

Overall, gradients are a great way to add depth and dimension to your designs in Adobe Illustrator, and they can be used in various ways, from simple background fills to complex texture overlays.

TRANSPARENCY AND BLENDING MODES

Transparency and blending modes are advanced design features in Adobe Illustrator that allow you to create complex and dynamic designs. Here's how you can use transparency and blending modes in Illustrator:

Transparency:

1. In a situation whereby you have two or more objects together, select the object you want to make transparent. In the image below, the circle will be selected and made to become transparent.

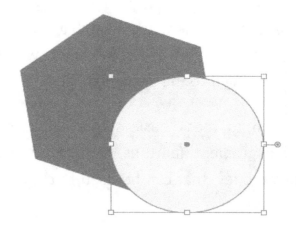

2. Open the Transparency panel by going to Window > Transparency.

3. Adjust the opacity of the object using the Opacity slider in the Transparency panel. You can also adjust the opacity of individual colors within the object by selecting the color and adjusting the opacity. Below is the result at 50%.

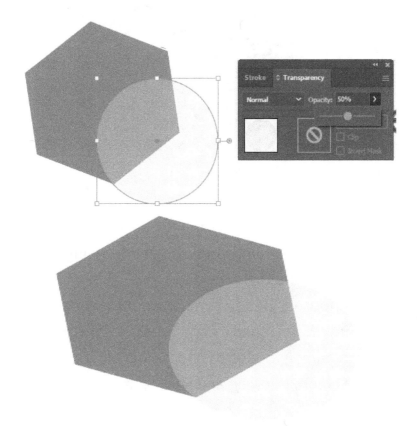

4. Apply a mask if you want to create a transparent effect in a specific area. To do this, select the object you want to mask, and choose Object > Clipping Mask > Make.

Blending modes:

1. Select the two objects you want to blend.

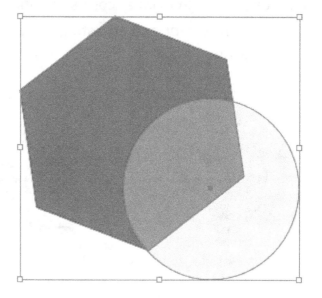

2. Open the Transparency panel by going to Window > Transparency.
3. Choose a blending mode from the drop-down menu in the Transparency panel. There are several blending modes to choose from, including Multiply, Screen, Overlay, and Soft Light.

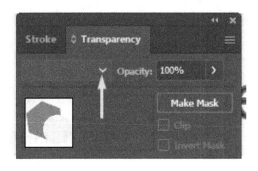

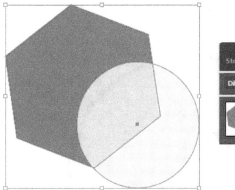
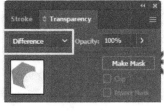

4. Adjust the opacity of the top object if necessary using the Opacity slider in the Transparency panel.

Blending modes can be used to create various effects in Illustrator, from adding texture and depth to creating complex color overlays. By combining transparency and blending modes, you can make even more advanced effects to bring your designs to life.

Overall, transparency and blending modes are powerful design tools in Adobe Illustrator that can be used to create unique and eye-catching designs. With some experimentation and practice, you can use these features to take your designs to the next level.

USING THE PAINTBRUSH TOOL

The Paintbrush Tool allows you to create unique and customizable lines and strokes.

To use the Paintbrush Tool in Adobe Illustrator, follow these steps:

1. Open Adobe Illustrator and create a new document.

2. Select the Paintbrush Tool from the Tools panel on the left side of the screen (shortcut key: B).

3. Choose a brush from the Brushes panel (Window > Brushes), or create a new brush by clicking on the New Brush button at the bottom of the panel.

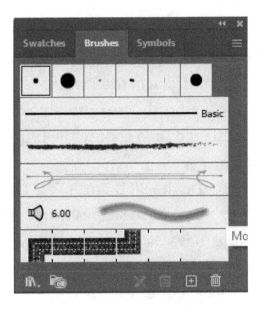

4. Click and drag on the canvas to create a stroke with the brush. You can adjust the size, shape, angle, and other settings of the brush stroke using the Brush Options dialog box.
5. To edit the brush stroke, use the Direct Selection Tool (shortcut key: A) to select the stroke, and then

use the various tools in the Tools panel to modify the stroke's appearance.

6. You can also use the Brush Tool to draw freehand shapes and lines by clicking and dragging on the canvas.

7. Experiment with different brushes and settings to create unique and customized brush strokes for your designs.

Tips:

- You can adjust the opacity and blending modes of the brush stroke in the Transparency panel.
- To apply a brush stroke to an existing path, select the path and then choose the brush from the Brush panel.
- You can use the Blob Brush Tool (shortcut key: Shift + B) to create filled shapes with the brush stroke.
- If you have a drawing tablet with pressure sensitivity, you can use it to control the size and opacity of your brush strokes.

The Brush Tool in Adobe Illustrator is a powerful tool that can help you create unique and customized artwork. By experimenting with different brush settings and applying them to your designs, you can create a wide variety of effects and styles.

THE ERASER, SCISSORS, AND KNIFE TOOLS

The Eraser, Scissors, and Knife tools are three valuable tools that can help you edit and manipulate your artwork in different ways.

Here's a brief overview of each tool:

1. Eraser Tool: The Eraser Tool allows you to erase parts of your artwork or paths. To use the Eraser Tool, select it from the Tools panel on the left side of the screen (shortcut key: Shift + E) and click and drag over the area you want to erase. You can also use the Eraser Tool to erase parts of a path by selecting the path and then clicking and dragging over it.

2. Scissors Tool: The Scissors Tool allows you to cut paths into multiple segments. To use the Scissors Tool, select it from the Tools panel (shortcut key: C) and click on the path where you want to cut it. You can then use the Direct Selection Tool to select and manipulate the segments of the path.

3. Knife Tool: The Knife Tool allows you to cut paths into freeform shapes. Select the Knife Tool from the Tools panel (shortcut key: Shift + K) and click and

drag over the path where you want to cut it. You can also hold down the Alt/Option key while dragging to make a straight cut.

Tips:

- You can use the Eraser Tool to create custom shapes by erasing parts of existing shapes.
- To use the Scissors Tool on a closed path, select the path and then choose the Scissors Tool. Click on the path where you want to cut it, and then click on the starting point to close the path again.
- The Knife Tool works best on simple paths without many curves or anchor points.
- You can use the Scissors Tool and Knife Tool together to create complex shapes and paths.

EXERCISE

This exercise is designed to help you practice adding colors and effects to basic shapes in Adobe Illustrator. As you become more comfortable with these techniques, you can experiment with more complex designs and effects.

1. Create a basic shape: Use the Shape Tool to create a basic shape, such as a square, circle, or triangle.

2. Add a gradient: Select the shape and click on the Gradient Tool. Click and drag the tool across the shape to add a gradient effect. Experiment with different colors and angles to create a unique gradient.

3. Add a stroke: Click on the Stroke Tool and choose a stroke color and weight. Click on the shape to add a stroke around the edge.

4. Add a drop shadow: Select the shape and click on the Effect menu. Choose Stylize and then Drop Shadow. Adjust the settings to create a subtle or dramatic drop shadow effect.

5. Add a texture: Download a texture image from a free stock photos website, such as Unsplash or Pexels. Drag the image into your Illustrator document and place it over the shape. Right-click on the image and choose Make Clipping Mask to mask the texture to the shape.

6. Add a 3D effect: Click on the shape and choose Effect, 3D, and Extrude & Bevel. Adjust the settings to create a 3D effect on the shape.

PART 5 → EXPORTING AND SAVING ADOBE ILLUSTRATOR FILES

Exporting a file involves converting the file from one format to another for use in another program or device. It may include modifying the file to make it suitable for its intended use.

Saving a file involves preserving the changes made to a file and storing them on a computer or other storage device. When you save a file, you give it a name and choose a location to store it on your computer. It is essential to save your work frequently to avoid losing any changes due to unforeseen events.

FILE FORMATS AND THEIR DIFFERENCES

Adobe Illustrator supports several file formats, each with its characteristics and uses. Here are some of the most common file formats used in Adobe Illustrator and their differences:

1. AI: This is the native file format of Adobe Illustrator. It allows you to save all the elements and properties of your artwork, including layers, paths, and effects.

2. PDF: This file format is widely used for sharing documents across different platforms and devices. PDF files can contain text, images, and vector graphics, making them useful for documents that require high-quality graphics.

3. EPS: Encapsulated PostScript (EPS) files are commonly used for printing, especially in the publishing industry. They can contain vector graphics, text, and images, and are often used to create logos and other types of graphics.

4. SVG: Scalable Vector Graphics (SVG) files are a web standard for vector graphics. They can be scaled without losing quality and are ideal for web graphics, logos, and icons.

5. JPG: Joint Photographic Experts Group (JPEG) files are a standard file format for photographs and other complex images. They use compression to reduce file size, but this can result in a loss of quality.

6. PNG: Portable Network Graphics (PNG) files are also commonly used for web graphics. They support transparency and can be saved with or without compression, making them ideal for logos and other types of graphics.

These file formats have different characteristics and are used for different purposes, so choosing the correct format is important depending on how you plan to use the file.

SAVING FILES IN DIFFERENT FORMATS

To save files in different formats in Adobe Illustrator, follow these steps:

1. Open your Illustrator file.
2. Click "File" in the top menu and select "Save As".
3. Choose a location to save the file and give it a name.
4. Select the file format you want to save it as from the "Save as type" dropdown menu.

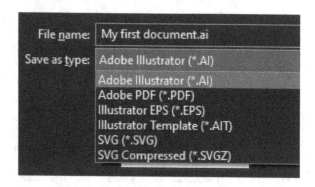

5. Choose any additional options or settings to apply to the file, such as resolution or compression.
6. Click "Save" to save the file in the selected format.

EXPORTING FILES FOR PRINT AND WEB

When exporting files for print and web in Adobe Illustrator, you need to consider the differences in color modes, resolution, and file formats. Here are some tips for exporting files for print and web:

For print:

1. Set the color mode to CMYK (Cyan, Magenta, Yellow, and Key/Black) for accurate color reproduction in print.
2. Use a high resolution of at least 300 DPI (dots per inch) to ensure the images and graphics appear sharp and clear.
3. Save the file in an EPS or PDF format, commonly used in print.

For web:

1. Set the color mode to RGB (Red, Green, and Blue) for accurate screen color representation.
2. Use a lower resolution of 72 DPI to reduce the file size and improve web page loading times.
3. Save the file in a PNG or JPG format, commonly used for web graphics.

When exporting for print or web, consider any specific requirements or guidelines provided by the printer or web developer. Additionally, previewing your exported file to ensure it looks as intended before sending it off for print or uploading it to the web is always a good idea.

Here are some steps to export files in Adobe Illustrator:

1. Open the Illustrator file you want to export.
2. Click on "File" in the top menu, select "Export" and select "Export As".
3. Choose a location to save the file and give it a name.
4. Select the file format you want to export from the "Save as type" dropdown menu.
5. Choose any additional options or settings to apply to the file, such as resolution or compression.
6. Click "Export" to export the file in the selected format.

Some standard file formats for exporting files from Adobe Illustrator include EPS, PDF, SVG, PNG, and JPG. The format you choose will depend on the intended use of the file, such as print, web, or digital media. Each format has its characteristics and uses, so it's important to choose the correct format depending on how you plan to use the file.

CREATING AND SAVING PRESETS

In Adobe Illustrator, you can quickly create and save presets to apply settings to new documents or artwork. Presets can be saved for various settings, such as document size, color mode, grids, and guides. Here are the steps to create and save presets in Adobe Illustrator:

1. Open Illustrator and create a new document or open an existing one.
2. Set up the settings you want to save as a preset, such as the document size, units of measurement, color mode, and other preferences.
3. Go to the "File" menu and select "Save As Template" or "Save Document Preset".
4. Enter a name for the preset and choose a location to save it to.
5. Click "Save" to save the preset.

To apply a preset to a new document, follow these steps:

1. Go to the "File" menu and select "New from Template" to create a new document.
2. Choose the preset you want to apply from the list.
3. Click "New" to create a new document with the preset settings.

Using presets can save you time and ensure consistency across your artwork and documents. You can also modify and delete presets as needed.

PART 6 → CONCLUSION, NEXT STEPS, AND EXERCISES

In this conversation, we covered some important concepts for beginners using Adobe Illustrator, including the basics of creating and manipulating shapes, working with colors and gradients, and applying text and typography. We also discussed some tips for exporting and saving files, as well as creating and saving presets.

If you are new to Adobe Illustrator, your next steps include exploring some of the different tools and features available in the program. You can find many online resources and tutorials to help you learn more about the software and improve your skills.

Here are some specific steps you might want to take as a beginner in Adobe Illustrator:

1. Practice creating basic shapes and experimenting with different fill and stroke colors.
2. Learn how to use the Pen tool to create custom shapes and paths.
3. Try creating and applying gradients to your shapes to add depth and dimension.

4. Experiment with different text options and learn how to format and style your text.

5. Explore the different panels and tools available in Illustrator, such as the Layers panel, the Appearance panel, and the Color panel.

6. Practice exporting and saving your files in different formats, and consider creating presets for your most commonly used settings.

With practice and patience, you can become proficient in using Adobe Illustrator and unlock its full potential for your design and illustration needs.

RECAP OF ADOBE ILLUSTRATOR BASICS

Here is a recap of some of the basic concepts we covered for Adobe Illustrator:

1. Illustrator is a vector graphics software for creating and editing scalable artwork.

2. The workspace in Illustrator includes various panels, tools, and menus for creating and editing artwork.

3. Basic shapes can be created using the shape tools, and custom shapes can be made using the Pen tool.

4. Colors can be applied to shapes using the fill and stroke options, and gradients can be used to add depth and dimension.

5. Text can be added and formatted using the Type tool and the Character and Paragraph panels.
6. Layers can be used to organize artwork and adjust the visibility and ordering of objects.
7. Files can be exported and saved in various formats, such as EPS, PDF, SVG, PNG, and JPG.
8. Presets can be created and saved to apply settings to new documents or artwork quickly.

These are just some of the basic concepts in Adobe Illustrator, and there is much more to explore and learn as you become more familiar with the software.

TIPS AND TRICKS FOR EFFICIENT WORKFLOW

Here are some tips and tricks for an efficient workflow in Adobe Illustrator:

1. Use keyboard shortcuts to save time: Learning and using keyboard shortcuts can speed up your workflow significantly. For example, pressing "V" on your keyboard will switch to the Selection tool, while pressing "T" will switch to the Type tool.
2. Customize your workspace: Arrange your panels and tools in a way that makes sense to you and maximizes your productivity. You can also save and switch between different workspace layouts.

3. Use the Appearance panel: The Appearance panel allows you to apply multiple fills and strokes to a single object, and it also lets you apply various effects, such as shadows and gradients. This can help you create more complex artwork with fewer objects.

4. Organize your layers: Use descriptive names for your layers and group related objects together. This will make finding and editing specific elements in your artwork more accessible.

5. Use symbols and libraries: If you have elements you frequently use, such as logos or icons, you can create symbols or save them to a library for easy access in future projects.

6. Use the Pathfinder panel: The Pathfinder panel allows you to combine or subtract shapes to create complex shapes and cutouts. This can save you time when creating complex designs.

7. Use the Align panel: The Align panel allows you to align and distribute objects precisely. This can help you create a more polished and professional design look.

8. Use the Transform panel: The Transform panel allows you to precisely adjust the size, position, and rotation of objects. This can save you time and help you create more consistent designs.

By incorporating these tips and tricks into your workflow, you can save time and work more efficiently in Adobe Illustrator.

KEYBOARD SHORTCUTS AND THEIR USES

Here are some of the commonly used keyboard shortcuts in Adobe Illustrator along with their uses:

1. Selection Tool: V - This tool selects objects on the artboard.
2. Direct Selection Tool: A - This tool is used to select individual anchor points or path segments of an object.
3. Rectangle Tool: M - This tool is used to draw rectangular shapes.
4. Ellipse Tool: L - This tool draws circular or elliptical shapes.
5. Line Tool: \ - This tool is used to draw straight lines.
6. Pen Tool: P - This tool is used to draw and edit vector paths.
7. Type Tool: T - This tool is used to add text to the artboard.
8. Zoom In: Ctrl + + - This shortcut is used to zoom in on the artboard.
9. Zoom Out: Ctrl + - - This shortcut is used to zoom out on the artboard.

10. Undo: Ctrl + Z - This shortcut is used to undo the last action.
11. Redo: Ctrl + Shift + Z - This shortcut is used to redo the last action.
12. Copy: Ctrl + C - This shortcut is used to copy selected objects.
13. Paste: Ctrl + V - This shortcut is used to paste copied objects.
14. Duplicate: Ctrl + Shift + D - This shortcut duplicates selected objects.
15. Group: Ctrl + G - This shortcut is used to group selected objects.
16. Ungroup: Ctrl + Shift + G - This shortcut ungroups selected objects.
17. Save: Ctrl + S - This shortcut saves the current file.
18. Save As: Ctrl + Shift + S - This shortcut is used to save the current file under a new name.
19. Align Left: Ctrl + Shift + L - This shortcut is used to align selected objects to the left.
20. Align Right: Ctrl + Shift + R - This shortcut is used to align selected objects to the right.

These keyboard shortcuts can help you work more efficiently and quickly in Adobe Illustrator, allowing you to complete your design projects more effectively.

RESOURCES FOR FURTHER LEARNING

Here are some resources you can use to further your learning in Adobe Illustrator:

1. Adobe Illustrator Help Center: Adobe's official help center provides articles and tutorials on various topics, from essential tools to advanced techniques.
2. Adobe Creative Cloud YouTube channel: This channel offers a range of video tutorials on Adobe Illustrator and other Creative Cloud applications.
3. LinkedIn Learning: LinkedIn Learning offers courses on Adobe Illustrator taught by industry professionals, with topics ranging from basic skills to advanced techniques.
4. Skillshare: Skillshare offers a variety of courses on Adobe Illustrator, including studies on specific topics such as logo design or typography.
5. Adobe Community: Adobe's community forum allows you to connect with other Illustrator users and ask for help or advice.
6. Books: Many books are available on Adobe Illustrator, ranging from beginner guides to advanced technique books.

These resources can help you continue to learn and improve your skills in Adobe Illustrator.

EXERCISES

Here are a few exercises for you to practice using Adobe Illustrator:

1. Create a basic logo: Use simple shapes, lines, and text to create a basic logo for a fictional company. Experiment with different fonts and colors to create a unique design.
2. Trace an image: Find a simple image or drawing online, and use the Pen Tool to trace over the lines and shapes in the image. You can then fill the shapes with color and adjust the stroke weight to create a more polished look.
3. Create a pattern: Use the Shape and Transform tools to create a simple pattern, such as a repeating geometric shape or a floral design. Experiment with different colors and shapes to create a visually interesting pattern.
4. Design a business card: Use the Rectangle Tool and Type Tool to create a basic business card design. You can also add a logo or other graphic elements to make the design more visually appealing.
5. Create a poster: Use a combination of text, images, and shapes to create a simple poster design for an event or product. Experiment with different fonts, colors, and layouts to create an eye-catching design.

6. Draw a character: Use the Pen Tool and other Shape tools to draw a simple cartoon character. Add color and shading to give the character more depth and personality.

These exercises are designed to help beginners get comfortable with the basic tools and techniques in Adobe Illustrator. As you become more comfortable with the software, you can experiment with more complex designs and techniques.